Brother Lawrence
A Christian Zen Master

Brother Lawrence
A Christian Zen Master

Anamchara Books

Copyright © 2011 by Anamchara Books,
a Division of Harding House Publishing Service, Inc.
All rights reserved. No part of this publication may be reproduced or transmitted in any form or by any means, electronic or mechanical, including photocopying, recording, taping, or any information storage and retrieval system, without permission from the publisher.

Anamchara Books
Vestal, NY 13850

9 8 7 6 5 4 3 2

Paperback ISBN: 978-1-933630-97-7
ebook ISBN: 978-1-933630-12-0

Library of Congress Control Number 2010918987

Interior and cover design by MK Bassett-Harvey.
Cover image © Mike Monahan / Dreamstime.com
Printed in the United States of America.

Contents

Introduction 7
God's Presence 13
Surrender 19
Self-Awareness 33
Spiritual Practice 39
Mindfulness 65
Mistakes, Doubts, & Worries 71
Work 81
Direction 91
Religion 95
Love 103
Notes on the Buddhist Teachers 109

Introduction

Brother Lawrence was a Carmelite monk born in France in the early years of the seventeenth century. He was no great intellectual, and he left behind neither a detailed biography nor any great theological treatise. In fact, we know only a handful of personal facts about the man: he felt guilty for failures he never described; he considered himself to be clumsy and awkward; and for all his ordinariness and humility, something about his life attracted the attention of others.

He began life as Nicholas Herman, an ordinary young man whose poverty drove him to join the army, where he received his meals and a small stipend. He soon had to leave the army, however, because of an injury (one that may have left him with a limp for the rest of his life). Eventually, he entered the Carmelite monastery in Paris as Brother Lawrence of the Resurrection.

There he complied with his superiors' instructions regarding prayer time; he read the spiritual books he was told to read. Neither activity brought him as great an awareness of God as had the stark branches of a tree in winter that had brought about his conversion. The world of the intellect had little interest for him, and he was not much concerned with theology or doctrine.

Brother Lawrence worked in the monastery's kitchen, however, and there, in the midst of the most ordinary and menial responsibilities, he developed an unusual and practical ability to focus himself on the presence of God. His simple awareness of the Divine Presence changed him. He was no longer overwhelmed with shame and self-loathing. Instead, he lived a life of such serenity and joy that others wanted to know his secret. He even attracted the attention of a cardinal.

The cardinal sent his envoy, the Abbe de Beaufort, to interview Brother Lawrence. Afterward, the abbe wrote a terse summary of Brother Lawrence's responses to his questions. This record, a few notes referred to as maxims, and a handful of letters were all Brother Lawrence left behind when he died at the age of eighty.

These sparse paragraphs were put together and became *The Practice of the Presence of God*, a small inspirational book that would continue to be read over the next three hundred years. Today, in the twenty-first century, it continues to challenge readers to understand the spiritual life in a new way.

More than eleven centuries before Brother Lawrence, another monk named Bodhidharma had developed a way of life that was not so different from that practiced by the Carmelite monk. Bodhidharma, however, was a Buddhist monk from India. He traveled through Southeast Asia and into China, bringing with him his teachings, creating a new understanding of Buddhism.

His teachings were, according to later sacred writings, "a special transmission outside the scriptures, not founded upon words and letters, by pointing directly to the mind." He taught that by focusing on the interior being, a person could wake up to the truth and light. Today, he is credited with being the father of Zen Buddhism.

The word "Zen" comes from a Sanskrit word that has to do with quieting or focusing the mind. It is the experience of being able to see truly, so that you no longer mistake your own identity with the world of circumstances, while at the same time you are more truly present in each moment, rather than living somewhere else, in either the past or the future. Zen itself is not a religion but a technique, a practice that can be applied to any religious tradition. However, it grew out of Buddhism, and it has always fit most comfortably within the Buddhist faith.

As a religion, Buddhism encompasses a wide range of traditions, beliefs, and practices, all based on the teachings of Siddhartha Gautama, who lived and taught in India somewhere between the sixth and fourth centuries BCE. He is known today as the Buddha, the awakened one. A simplistic understanding of Buddhism equates Buddha with God, but Buddha made no claim to be divine.

In fact, according to Buddhist scriptures, when one of his students asked him if he were the messiah, he answered, "No."

"Then are you a healer?" the student persisted.

"No."

"Then are you a teacher?"

"No, I am not a teacher."

"Then what are you?" By this time the student was exasperated.

"I am awake," Buddha replied.

This state of being awake, of being enlightened—totally present in the light—is the goal of Buddhism.

So what does this have to do with a seventeenth-century Christian monk?

At its heart, Brother Lawrence's practice was simply Zen—a focus on the present moment in order to wake up, to be able to see the Light. This way of living drew not only the attention of church leaders during his day; down through the centuries, it has continued to draw the attention of those who see in Brother Lawrence's life a way of relating to God that Christianity has often neglected. Other mystics, including Meister Eckhart and Teresa of Avila, might be able to explain this in greater detail in their writing; Brother Lawrence simply lived it.

Not all Christians have welcomed this perspective. Over the years, many have condemned Brother Lawrence for a dangerous lack of doctrine, for focusing on simply being rather than understanding and obeying the Bible. (Interestingly, many traditional Buddhists looked at Zen with the same fear and suspicion.)

Christianity and Buddhism may find it difficult to communicate because they use very different vocabularies, separate lexicons for talking about the meaning of Reality. Their words seem mutually exclusive. How can we say that a person like Brother Lawrence, passionately in love with Jesus

Christ, has anything to do with the cool, almost bloodless serenity of Zen?

As Christians, however, we may simply be confused by Zen's unfamiliar terminology. Zen asks us to let go of our focus on the ego, to empty ourselves of our selfish attachments, to destroy our mental constructs, and simply be present to the light. Not so very different from Christ's call to die to ourselves so that we may be born again! According to Brother David Steindl-Rast, "Christians need to think 'Nothing' when they call God 'Love.' Buddhists need to think 'Love' when they say 'Emptiness.' This will at least wake us up to the fact that words must always fall short of the ineffable."

In this book, you will find modern-language paraphrases from *The Practice of the Presence of God*, paired with writings from many different Buddhist teachers, divided into sections based on common themes. These couplings are not meant to demonstrate a one-to-one correspondence, nor are they intended to prove that Zen Buddhism and Christianity (or at least Brother Lawrence's version of it) are one and the same. They are not. But one can shine light on the other.

We have all had the experience of seeing a familiar face in an unfamiliar setting, so that we are taken by surprise, startled out of our familiarity. For an instant, we may not even recognize the person we thought we knew so well—and when we do, we see that person in a new way, with a fresh awareness. As Christians, a similar thing can happen when we look at our own faith from a different direction. The experience can be uncomfortable, but it can shake us free of what we think we know and confront us with a deeper truth. Ultimately, it can bring a richer life to our faith.

According to a Zen teaching, if you meet the Buddha on the road, you should kill him. This seemingly brutal and nonsensical statement reminds us to beware of trying to confine our faith within tidy mental boxes. When we do so, we create false gods. We cling to the image, the face we take for granted we know so well, and we miss the reality.

Brother Lawrence shows us a new face for Christianity. By holding his words up to the light of Buddhist teachers, that face may become even more unfamiliar. It may ask us to kill the Christianity we thought we knew—so that we can enter the Presence of God.

Anne Morrow Lindbergh wrote of living "like a child or saint in the immediacy of the here and now." It is the present moment, this fleeting *now*, where we too touch the God who names the Divine Selfhood as present-tense being: I AM. This is the Presence that Brother Lawrence of the Resurrection experienced nearly four centuries ago. Zen practice allows us to know this Presence, to enter it, to give it our full attention: *now*.

"Absolute attention," wrote Simone Weil, "is prayer."

God's Presence

Brother Lawrence, A Christian Zen Master

The winter I was eighteen, I stood looking at the bare branches of a tree. I realized that in time the leaves would grow again, and then flowers would bloom on the branches, followed by fruit. My awareness was suddenly opened, so that I saw God's great strength and care. That realization has never since been erased from my mind. This new understanding cut my ties to the world, and it lit in me such a great love for God that I cannot tell whether it has increased over the course of the more than forty years I have lived since that moment when I stood looking at the tree's naked branches.

> Mountains and rivers, the whole earth—
> All manifest forth the essence of being.
> The old pine-tree speaks divine wisdom.
>
> —Zenrinkushu

God's Presence

We can keep ourselves balanced and stable by maintaining a sense of God's Presence—and we do this by continually talking to God. When we end our conversation with God by thinking of trivial nonsense and idle untruths, we cloud our hearts. Feed and nourish your soul with thoughts of God.

> We are shaped by our thoughts;
>
> we become what we think.
>
> When the mind is pure,
>
> joy follows like a shadow that never leaves.
>
> —the Buddha

Brother Lawrence A Christian Zen Master

I can't always maintain my focus on God, of course. I'll suddenly discover that I've barely given God a thought for a good long while. Usually, what gets my attention is that I'll notice how wretched I'm feeling—and then I'll realize I've forgotten God's presence. But I don't worry about it much. I just turn back to God immediately. And having realized how miserable I am when I forget God, my trust in God is always that much greater.

> When the moon sets, people say that the moon has disappeared; and when the moon rises, they say that the moon has appeared. In fact, the moon neither goes nor comes, but shines continually in the sky. Buddha is exactly like the moon: He neither appears nor disappears; He only seems to do so out of love for the people that He may teach them.
>
> —Mahaparinirvana Sutra

The practice of the Divine Presence is a natural and ongoing conversation with God, one that constantly occupies our minds with love and adoration for the infinite perfection of God.

> There is a tremendous difference between loneliness and aloneness.
> . . . Loneliness is a negative state.
> . . . Aloneness is very positive.
> It is a presence, overflowing presence.
>
> —Osho

The Divine Presence occupies the here and now. If you are not aware of this— become so!

> To live fully is to let go and die with each passing moment, and to be reborn in each new one.
>
> —Jack Kornfield

Brother Lawrence A Christian Zen Master

In some sense, God is nearer to us
when we are in pain
than when we are healthy.

> Suffering chastens us and
> makes us remember.
>
> —Buddhadhasa Bhikku

God is within you. Don't look for the
Divine Presence anywhere else.

> The Buddha is as near to
> you as your own heart.
>
> —Ayya Khema

Surrender

Brother Lawrence A Christian Zen Master

I thought I deserved to be punished,
and so I sacrificed my life and
pleasures on God's altar. But God
disappointed me! Instead of punishment, I have found nothing but
satisfaction and pleasure.

> One of the Buddha's students said to him:
> "A person who has children
> delights in children,
> one with cattle delights in cattle.
> Acquisitions are truly a person's delight."
> The Buddha answered:
> "The person who has children
> sorrows over children,
> one with cattle sorrows over cattle.
> Acquisitions truly are a person's sorrows;
> without acquisitions, you do not sorrow.
> When you have abandoned all,
> that will lead to your welfare and happiness."

Surrender yourself to God and you
will find great joy.
If you have truly surrendered yourself,
you will be equally at peace in both
suffering and pleasure.

> When a person does not cling,
> she is not agitated.
>
> —the Buddha

The way of faith—total surrender—
will lead us to completion;
it will show us how to achieve our full
development.

> If he comes we welcome.
> If he goes we do not pursue.
>
> —Zen saying

Brother Lawrence A Christian Zen Master

If we give up ourselves to God,
offering our being to God in both the
temporary experiences of this world
as well as in the spiritual realm, we
will find our satisfaction in fulfilling
God's will.

> *Experiences are not realization*
> *in themselves;*
> *but if we remain free of attachment to them,*
> *they become what they really are—*
> *that is, materials for realization.*
>
> —Sogyal Rinpoche

Surrender

This world's pleasures and pains
cannot compare to the joy that comes
from spiritual surrender. Since that's
the case, why should I worry about
anything? All I want is God. I have let
go of everything else.

> All the violence, fear and
> suffering in this world
> comes from grasping at "self."
> What use is this great monster to you?
> If you do not let go of the "self,"
> there will never be an end to your suffering.
>
> —Shantideva

Trust—the total surrender of all we
are—makes room in our lives for
God's grace. And God's grace is that
which brings us continual joy.

> Realizations come naturally
> through the practice of surrendering.
>
> —Jae Woong Kim

If we make a sincere surrender of
everything in our lives that does not
lead us to God, then we will be able to
be in constant conversation with God,
with total freedom and simplicity.

> Unless we have the determination
> to increase our mindfulness
> from moment to moment,
> we will easily forget to practice it.
>
> —Ayya Khema

Surrender

We start our spiritual journey by being willing to deny ourselves. But after a while, you forget all about denial and sacrifice, because your life is so full of indescribable delight. Any time our road seems difficult, all we have to do is turn to Jesus Christ and ask for His grace—and then everything becomes easy again.

> Although we have been made to believe
> that if we let go we will end up with nothing,
> life itself reveals again and again the opposite:
> that letting go is the path to real freedom.
>
> —Sogyal Rinpoche

Brother Lawrence A Christian Zen Master

I have let go of everything else,
and so I pass my life in total
joy. Make a decision, once and
for all, to do the same: let your
entire self drop into God's hands,
confident that God will never let
you fall.

> The recollected go forth to
> lives of renunciation.
> They take no pleasure in a fixed abode.
> Like wild swans abandoning a pool,
> they leave one resting place after another.
>
> —the Buddha

Surrender

I made up my mind to give my all to the All. I have surrendered all that is not God. I live as though God and I are alone in the world.

> Whatever is material shape,
> past, future, present;
> subjective or objective; gross or subtle;
> mean or excellent, whether it is far or near—
> all material shape should be seen by
> perfect intuitive wisdom as it really is:
> "This is not mine, this I am
> not, this is not my self."
>
> —the Buddha

Brother Lawrence A Christian Zen Master

I am like a stone in a carver's hands.
I surrender myself totally,
so that God can create the Divine
image in my soul,
making me entirely like God.

> Enlightenment is like the moon
> reflected on the water. . . .
> Although its light is wide and great,
> the moon is reflected even in
> a puddle an inch wide.
> The whole moon and the entire sky
> are reflected in one dewdrop on the grass.
>
> —Dogen

Surrender

Empty yourself.
Leave your heart vacant.
Only then will there be room for God.

*Die each moment,
so that you can be new each moment.*

—*Osho*

Use whatever life brings you—
even physical sickness—
as an opportunity to practice surrender. When you do, your pain will be
anointed and filled with peace.

*You suffer because you don't want to accept
what has to be accepted.*

—*Sawaki Kôdô Rôshi*

When you suffer, accept your pain.
Do not fight against it. Surrender
to it. Allow God to be the nails
that hold you to your cross. Make
a habit of facing pain in this way,
and you will no longer see pain as
something that goes against nature,
something that causes you emotional distress. Accept your pain as
coming from the Divine hand, and
you will be able to use it as a means
for growth and wholeness. Rely on
God for your recovery.

> Do not hope or pray to be exempt from
> sickness. Without sickness, desires and
> passions can easily arise. . . . While acting
> in society, do not hope or pray not to
> have any difficulties. Without difficulties,
> arrogance can easily arise. . . . While
> meditating on the mind, do not hope or
> pray not to encounter hindrances.

Without hindrances, present knowledge
will not be challenged or broadened. . . .
While working, do not hope or pray not to
encounter obstacles. Without obstacles, the
vow to help others will not deepen.
. . . While interacting with others, do not
hope or pray to gain personal profit. With
the hope for personal gain, the spiritual
nature of the encounter is diminished. . . .
While speaking with others, do not hope
or pray not to be disagreed with. Without
disagreement, self-righteousness can
flourish. . . . The Buddha spoke of sickness
and suffering as effective medicines.
Times of difficulties and accidents are
also times of freedom and realization.
Obstacles can be a form of liberation.

—Thich Nhat Hanh

Don't worry about whether circumstances are "bad" or "good." Instead, accept them equally as Divine gifts. When you change your perspective in this way, you will see in a new light. Pain will no longer be bitter. Life's challenges will no longer be unbearable.

> A monk asked,
> "How shall we practice in the heat of summer or the cold of winter?"
> The master answered,
> "Simply practice in the spot where it is neither hot nor cold."
> "But where is such spot?"
> "When heat comes, die to the heat, when cold comes, die to the cold."
>
> —Buddhist koan

Self-Awareness

Brother Lawrence A Christian Zen Master

Pay attention to your emotions, including the ones that mingle with your spiritual life, as well as the ones that seem more connected to ordinary life. If you really want to serve God, then you will find the light you need to understand your emotions.

> There's a difference between
> watching the mind
> and controlling the mind.
> Watching the mind with a
> gentle, open attitude
> allows the mind to settle down and rest.
> Trying to control the mind,
> or trying to control the way that
> one's spiritual practice unfolds,
> just stirs up more agitation and suffering.
>
> —Bhante Henepola Gunaratana

Self-Awareness

Whenever you enter the spiritual realm, take a close look at yourself. Examine your thoughts and feelings, seeking out the very bottom level of who you are. You will become aware of all that pains you; you will see how circumstances have troubled you, both internally and externally; you will realize how your physical health and your emotions have been changed as a result of all that God has allowed to come into your life. If you practice this perspective, you will no longer resent the trials and frustrations that come into your life. Instead, you will learn to surrender yourself to them, accepting them as gifts from God, allowing them to do their work on your being.

> Cast off everything and just sit,
> making the self into the self.
>
> —Uchiyami Rôshi

Brother Lawrence A Christian Zen Master

When you realize the treasure you can find in yourself, you no longer need to search anxiously for it outside yourself. This treasure chest is always open, and you may take what you please from it.

> *Everything has its own identity,*
> *which is unsurpassable in*
> *the whole universe.*
>
> — Sawaki Kôdô Rôshi

Self-Awareness

Enter into yourself and break down all that hinders the flow of God's grace. Don't waste time. I say it again: enter into yourself. If you do not go forward, you will go backward. But those who are blown by the winds of the Holy Spirit will go forward even in their sleep. If your soul's ship is tossed by storms, wake the Divine One who rests within your being. God will calm the sea.

> To study the Way is to study the self.
> To study the self is to forget the self.
> To forget the self is to be
> Enlightened by all things.
>
> —Dogen

Spiritual Practice

God tests our love by sending us times when prayer seems dry or pointless or tiresome. But if we remain committed to prayer during those times—especially during those times—we grow spiritually.

> When we practice prayers or meditations,
> it may look like we are alone,
> like we are practicing for ourselves,
> but we are not practicing for ourselves,
> and we are not alone.
>
> —Nyoshul Khenpo Rinpoche
> and Lama Surya Das

Spiritual Practice

If I so much as pick up something that's dropped on the ground, I find joy in doing it for God. I seek only God, nothing else, not even the Divine gifts.

> Once an old woman came to Buddha and asked him how to meditate. He told her to remain aware of every movement of her hands as she drew water from the well, knowing that if she did, she would soon find herself in that state of alert and spacious calm that is meditation.
>
> —Sogyal Rinpoche

Brother Lawrence A Christian Zen Master

I see no difference between set times of prayer and the rest of my life. My Superior here at the monastery tells me to go to my cell to pray at certain times of the day, so I do—but I don't need those times to maintain my prayer life. No matter how busy I am, I'm always focused on God. Life no longer distracts me. Instead, each task, no matter how small, is like a prayer bead that focuses my attention on God.

> *If you have time to be mindful,
> you have time to meditate.*
>
> —Ajahn Chah

My thoughts are the biggest obstacles to this way of living my life. The little useless thoughts that drift through my head, making mischief, distracting me. I've learned to reject them as soon as I notice them. They have nothing to do with the reality at hand—nor with my eternal salvation—and once I stop paying attention to them, I can get back to communing with God.

> Everything is based on mind, is led
> by mind, is fashioned by mind.
> If you speak and act with a polluted mind,
> suffering will follow you, as the
> wheels of the oxcart
> follow the footsteps of the ox. . . .
> If you speak and act with a pure mind,
> happiness will follow you, as a
> shadow clings to a form.
>
> —the Buddha

Brother Lawrence A Christian Zen Master

I don't practice any particular prayer discipline. I have no specific technique I use to meditate. I know these methods work for many people. But for me, when I tried them, I just spent all my time rejecting my wandering thoughts, over and over. I've tried to practice these disciplines, but now I don't worry about them anymore. Their only purpose anyway is to bring a person to union with God. Why should I fast or set aside particular prayer times or deny myself in some way when I've found the shortcut? If every moment I'm consciously practicing love, doing all things for God's sake, then I don't need to worry about these spiritual methods.

> As long as there is definite ground on the spiritual quest, it becomes a struggle, a deliberate attitude of achievement. And once we begin to be aware of our process of searching as an ambitious struggle, that struggle automatically becomes a . . .

struggle with ideas, a struggle with theology, concept, . . . rather than the spiritual path. Emptiness is that which frees us from religiosity and leads us to true spirituality.

—Chogyam Trungpa

So many people fail to grow closer to Christ because they focus on penances and other particular disciplines, while they forget the thing for which they were created: to simply love God. You can always tell. People's actions give them away. Those whose hearts are filled with love for God will reveal themselves through their strength and kindness.

The mind of faith is pure and gentle, always patient and enduring, never causing suffering to others.

—the Buddha

Brother Lawrence A Christian Zen Master

You don't need some particular method for coming to God. It doesn't take a specific skill or course of study. All it requires is a heart that has resolutely committed itself to God, asking nothing in return but God alone.

> Sometimes when I meditate,
> I don't use any particular method.
> I just allow my mind to rest. . . .
> A fundamental trust is present.
> There is nothing in particular to do.
>
> —Sogyal Rinpoche

Spiritual Practice

The best spiritual practice I have found
is simply my ordinary, everyday work.
When I do my work for God, rather
than to impress others, my work
brings me to God.

> So the thing to do when working on a
> . . . task, is to cultivate the peace of mind
> which does not separate one's self from
> one's surroundings. When that is done
> successfully, then everything else follows
> naturally. Peace of mind produces right
> values, right values produce right thoughts.
> Right thoughts produce right actions and
> right actions produce work which will
> be a material reflection for others to see
> of the serenity at the center of it all.
>
> —Robert M. Pirsig

Brother Lawrence A Christian Zen Master

We should not set aside our prayer time as being different from the other hours in the day. If we do, we tend to assume that we need not cling as tightly to God in the active moments of our day, when we are busy with daily concerns. The reality is just the opposite. Times devoted to prayer may have their proper place in our lives—but we need to pay equally close attention to God's presence at all times, no matter what we are doing.

> To practice the way of Buddha
> means to completely live out
> this present moment—
> which is our whole life—here and now.
>
> —Sawaki Kôdô Rôshi

For me, prayer is nothing more than a sense of God's presence, an overwhelming awareness of Divine love. This awareness continues uninterrupted, both in prayer times and throughout the day. Why should we see any difference? God doesn't go away because we are not praying. That is why I continue to walk constantly with God, giving God all my strength.

> Even though the meditator may
> leave the meditation,
> the meditation will not leave the meditator.
>
> —Dudjom Rinpoche

Brother Lawrence A Christian Zen Master

At the beginning of my spiritual practice in the monastery, I used the hours set aside for private prayer to simply think about God. I wanted God's reality to imprint itself on my mind and emotions. I felt this was far more useful than any particular prayer practice or theological study. This method is short and sure. It allows me to exercise my knowledge and love for God, so that I am able to take my awareness of the Divine Presence with me, so that I never need to leave it.

> Carry your meditation as the eternal present, and saturate your everyday life with it.
>
> —Nyogen Senzaki

Spiritual Practice

I read in spiritual books many
different ways of praying. I heard
about various spiritual practices.
They only puzzled me. They didn't get
me any closer to that which I sought:
to become wholly surrendered to God.

> When ignorance is abandoned and
> true knowledge has arisen . . .
> he no longer clings to views,
> no longer clings to rules and observances,
> no longer clings to a doctrine of self.
> When he does not cling, he is not agitated.
>
> —the Buddha

Brother Lawrence A Christian Zen Master

I have abandoned all particular forms of devotion, all prayer techniques. My only prayer practice is attention. I carry on a habitual, silent, and secret conversation with God that fills me with overwhelming joy.

> The real glory of meditation
> lies not in any method
> but in its continual living
> experience of presence,
> in its bliss, clarity, peace, and,
> most important of all, complete
> absence of grasping.
>
> —Sugyal Rinpoche

Spiritual Practice

In prayer, I feel my spirit and soul rise effortlessly, suspended above this life, fixed in God, centered and at rest. Some consider this to be a state of inactivity, delusion, and self-love. And I admit that it is a holy inactivity, even a happy self-love, though the self in this state is incapable of selfishness. In fact, while the soul is in this state of rest, she cannot be disturbed by selfish thoughts. That which normally supports the self disappears; that which she once depended on would now only hold her back.

> You can't hold on to your self.
> The very moment you give your self up,
> you realize the self which is
> one with the universe.
>
> —Sawaki Kôdô Rôshi

Brother Lawrence A Christian Zen Master

It only takes a few short words, repeated throughout the day. "Make me according to Your heart, God. Make my thoughts Yours." And then the God of love rests in the depth and center of my soul. I cannot doubt that God is always there, at the very deepest level of my being.

> Human beings tend to move
> in the direction of their thoughts.
>
> —the Buddha

You don't need to go to church to find God. Your mind can be a place of prayer, a sanctuary where you retire from time to time.

> Make yourself your refuge.
> Walk in the world and be
> unchained from everything.
>
> —the Buddha

Don't be discouraged if you don't feel like being spiritual! At first, you will feel as though you are wasting time, but make up your mind to persevere for the rest of your life, no matter how many difficulties you encounter.

> This is practicing realization. . . . It is exactly as if we were told as babies, "From now on you will have to breathe, your whole life long, this very breath, again and again, every single moment. You will breathe in and breathe out billions of times." What baby would say, "Oh no! I've got to find some way to take care of these billion breaths once and for all, with one really big breath. . ."? Even if we tried, we would not succeed.
>
> —Uchiyama Kôshô Rôshi

Brother Lawrence A Christian Zen Master

God makes no great demands of us—
simply remember God from time to
time, occasionally offer up your sadness or pain, sometimes give thanks
for all you have even in the midst of
your troubles, and take comfort in
God as often as you can. Lift up your
heart to God, while you are eating,
while you are talking with others. God
will use the briefest moment.

> Each and every step is the goal.
>
> — Sawaki Kôdô Rôshi

You need not shout to get God's attention.
God is always nearer than you are aware.

> Don't strain. Don't force anything
> or make grand, exaggerated efforts.
> There is no place or need for violent striving.
> Just let your effort be relaxed and steady.
>
> —Bhante Henepola Gunaratana

Spiritual Practice

All of us are capable of carrying on
intimate conversations with God,
some of us more, some of us less.
God knows what we can do.

> Buddha has many forms of transfiguration
> and incarnation, and can manifest
> Himself in manifold ways
> according to the ability of each person.
>
> —the Buddha

The more you practice the presence
of God throughout your day,
the easier you will find it to
maintain your focus during your
prayer times.

> In the same way that rain breaks
> into a house with a bad roof,
> desire breaks into the mind that has
> not been practicing meditation.
>
> —the Buddha

Brother Lawrence *A Christian Zen Master*

You are not the only one who is troubled with wandering thoughts during times of prayer. Our minds scatter their arrows every which way, here and there, without a target. In the end, however, you can choose to carry all of them to God.

> *Isn't it extraordinary that our minds cannot stay still for longer than a few moments without grasping after distraction? . . . So many contradictory voices, dictates, and feelings fight for control over our inner lives that we find ourselves scattered everywhere, in all directions, leaving nobody at home. Meditation, then, is bringing the mind home.*
>
> —Sogyal Rinpoche

Spiritual Practice

Don't use lots of words when you pray.
Long discourses will only distract you;
you will lose your focus in all those
words. Instead, be like a beggar
who can neither speak nor move but
simply waits at the gate. Come silently,
without words, into the Divine Presence.

> You cry out, "Peace, peace!"
> but if you would only be quiet,
> it would be so much more peaceful.
>
> —Sawaki Kôdô Rôshi

An interior conversation with God will
give great pleasure—but that should not
be your motive. Do not seek pleasure. Seek
only love. The pleasure is only a side effect.

> You say you're seeking the way,
> but what does it mean if you're seeking the way
> just to satisfy yourself?
>
> —Sawaki Kôdô Rôshi

Brother Lawrence A Christian Zen Master

When your thoughts wander (as they will), don't worry about it, since worry will only distract you further. Bring yourself back to silence, to tranquility.

> In meditation, negative experiences are the most misleading, because we tend to take them as a bad sign. But in fact the negative experiences in our practice are blessings in disguise. Try to not react to them with aversion as you might normally do, but recognize them instead for what they truly are, merely experiences, illusory and dreamlike.
>
> —Sogyal Rinpoche

Spiritual Practice

When you begin a spiritual practice,
it is very difficult to stick with it.
But though it is difficult, persevere.
Surrender to God your sense of difficulty, your failure.
No matter how many years it takes,
keep surrendering, continue to
persevere.

> Sit silently for ten years,
> then for ten more years,
> and then for another ten years.
>
> —Uchiyama Kosho Rôshi

Brother Lawrence A Christian Zen Master

Don't do violence to yourself
by attempting to practice harsh and
extreme disciplines. Instead, serve
God in healthy freedom.

> Let me tell you about the middle path.
> Dressing in rough and dirty garments,
> letting your hair grow matted, abstaining
> from eating any meat or fish, does not
> cleanse the one who is deluded. Mortifying
> the flesh through excessive hardship does
> not lead to a triumph over the senses.
> All self-inflicted suffering is useless as
> long as the feeling of self is dominant.
> You should lose your involvement with
> yourself and then eat and drink naturally,
> according to the needs of your body.
> Attachment to your appetites—whether
> you deprive or indulge them—can lead to
> slavery, but satisfying the needs of daily
> life is not wrong. Indeed, to keep a body
> in good health is a duty, for otherwise
> the mind will not stay strong and clear.
>
> —the Buddha

Spiritual practices themselves may need to be laid aside. These practices are only intended to be means to an end. Don't become confused and think that the practices in and of themselves are worth anything! God's presence is our only goal, and love is the only currency we need.

> A method is only a means,
> not the meditation itself.
> It is through practicing the method skillfully
> that you reach the perfection
> of that pure state of total presence,
> which is the real meditation.
>
> —Sogyal Rinpoche

Brother Lawrence A Christian Zen Master

Each of us may have unique ways of seeking God's presence: one may sense God best through praise and adoration, another through surrender, yet another through yearning and emptiness, and still another through gratitude. Let your own spirit's invention guide you.

> Bring together your understanding of the essential nature of your mind, your knowledge of your various, shifting moods, and the insight you have developed through your practice into how to work with yourself, from moment to moment. By bringing these together, you learn the art of applying whatever method is appropriate to any particular situation or problem, to transform that environment of your mind.
>
> —Sogyal Rinpoche

Mindfulness

Brother Lawrence A Christian Zen Master

The habit of directing our attention constantly toward God takes a little effort at first, but as we make it a habit, Divine love works within us, calling out of us our commitment to God, until communicating with God becomes habitual and natural.

> He who meditates attentively
> attains abundant joy.
>
> —the Buddha

I do not live the way I do for any reason except for the love of God. Everything I do, I try to do for God. So whatever becomes of me after death, whether I am destroyed or kept safe for eternity, while I live here on Earth, I choose to act only in God's love—

Mindfulness

and that way, I can at least find joy in
this life, no matter what happens in
the next.

> If this elephant of mind is bound on all
> sides by the cord of mindfulness,
> All fear disappears and complete
> happiness comes.
> All enemies: all the tigers, lions, elephants,
> bears, serpents (of our emotions);
> And all the keepers of hell; the
> demons and the horrors,
> All of these are bound by the
> mastery of your mind,
> And by the taming of that one
> mind, all are subdued,
> Because from the mind are derived all
> fears and immeasurable sorrows.
>
> —Shantideva

Brother Lawrence *A Christian Zen Master*

Think of your thoughts as arrows.
Think of God as their target.

> It isn't enough to hit the bull's eye once.
> Last's year's perfect marks are useless.
> You've got to hit the bull's eye right now.
>
> —Sawaki Kôdô Rôshi

Pay attention.
Be mindful of God,
the way a nursing baby is aware only
of his mother's breast.
Taste God's sweetness.
Experience God's delight.
Rest on God's breasts.

> Since they are resting in the
> bosom of Buddha by faith,
> they are kept far from having a selfish mind.
>
> —Avatamsaka Sutra

Mindfulness

God has infinite treasure to bestow.
But our blindness gets in the way.
Our lack of awareness blocks the
Divine current of grace. And then
when we are open, aware, filled with
living faith, Divine grace pours into
us, a torrent that floods our life with
impetuous abundance.

> Everything can be used as an invitation to meditation. A smile, a face in the subway, the sight of a small flower growing in the crack of cement pavement, a fall of rich cloth in a shop window, the way the sun lights up flower pots on a windowsill. Be alert for any sign of beauty or grace. Offer up every joy, be awake at all moments, to "the news that is always arriving out of silence." Slowly, you will become a master of your own bliss, a chemist of your own joy, with all sorts of remedies always at hand to elevate, cheer, illuminate, and inspire your every breath and movement.
>
> —Sogyal Rinpoche

Mistakes, Doubts, & Worries

Brother Lawrence A Christian Zen Master

When I fail to turn to God the way
I should, when I let someone down,
I admit my mistake. And then I say
to God, "This is how things always
will turn out when I try to do things
on my own. You are the only one
who can keep me from falling—and
You are the only one who can mend
my mistakes." And once I've done
this, I put it out of my mind and stop
worrying about it.

> The secret of health for both mind and body
> is not to mourn for the past,
> not to worry about the future,
> nor to anticipate troubles,
> but to live the present moment
> wisely and earnestly.
>
> —the Buddha

Mistakes, Doubts, & Worries

I know I have many faults and failures, but I don't let them discourage me. I simply try to be as aware of them as I can be, and then I offer them up to God, without excuse. Once I've done that, I'm at peace again, and I can get on with my life's business: loving and adoring God.

> As you breathe in, accept total responsibility for your actions in that particular situation, without in any way trying to justify your behavior. Acknowledge exactly what you have done wrong, and wholeheartedly ask for forgiveness. Now, as you breathe out, send out reconciliation, forgiveness, healing, and understanding. So you breathe in blame, and breathe out the undoing of harm; you breathe in responsibility, breathe out healing, forgiveness, and reconciliation.
>
> —Sogyal Rinpoche

Brother Lawrence A Christian Zen Master

Since I'm perfectly willing to lay down
my life as an act of love for God,
why should I worry about any danger
this world can offer?

> Without attachment to their possessions,
> they have no fear in their daily life.
>
> —Avatamsaka Sutra

We need not be discouraged about our
failures, but instead rely with total
confidence on God's infinite abilities.

> Be gentle with yourself.
> Be kind to yourself.
> You may not be perfect,
> but you are all you've got to work with.
> The process of becoming who you will be
> begins first with the total
> acceptance of who you are.
>
> —Bhante Henepola Gunaratana

Go about your life without anxiety,
and no matter how many times your
mind wanders from God,
bring it back gently and peacefully.

> The solution is not to suppress our
> thoughts and desires, for this would
> be impossible; it would be like trying
> to keep a pot from boiling by pressing
> down tightly on the lid. The only sensible
> approach is to train ourselves to observe
> our thoughts without following them.
> This deprives them of their compulsive
> energy and is therefore like removing
> the pot of boiling water from the fire.
>
> —Lama Thubten Yeshe

Brother Lawrence A Christian Zen Master

Sometimes we are double-minded rather than focused, filled with doubt rather than trust. But don't worry. If we only seek to please God, Divine light will always shine into our doubts, uniting our thoughts into a single focus once more.

> When little obstacles crop up on the spiritual path, a good practitioner does not lose faith and begin to doubt, but has the discernment to recognize difficulties, whatever they may be, for what they are—just obstacles, and nothing more. It is the nature of things that when you recognize an obstacle as such, it ceases to be an obstacle. Equally, it is by failing to recognize an obstacle for what it is, and therefore taking it seriously, that it is empowered and solidified and becomes a real blockage.
>
> —Sogyal Rinpoche

Mistakes, Doubts, & Worries

I examine myself so I know when I
have failed to keep myself focused on
God. I don't get discouraged, though.
I simply set my mind right again, and
then I continue on in the practice
of the Divine Presence, as though I
had never slipped away from it. I get
back up immediately after my falls.
In doing so, my faith and love are
renewed—and at last, thinking of God
has become so habitual that I would
find it as difficult now *not* to think of
God as in the beginning it was hard to
get used to thinking about God.

> If we have said anything during
> the day that we now regret,
> we've lacked deliberation and lost mindfulness.
> There's no blame attached, only recognition.
>
> —Ayya Khema

Brother Lawrence *A Christian Zen Master*

Don't be surprised if at first you fail to
keep your focus on God.
Don't give up. After a while,
turning your thoughts toward God
will become a habit.
This habit will naturally lead to a
certain way of acting.
The habit will carry you along, effortlessly and delightfully.

There is no armor like perseverance.

—Buddhist saying

Mistakes, Doubts, & Worries

Don't try to go faster than grace can carry you. No one becomes whole all at once. Don't become so focused on your goal that you lose sight of God's presence now.

> In the beginner's mind there
> are many possibilities. . . .
> When we have no thought of achievement,
> no thought of self,
> we are true beginners. . . .
> Always be a beginner.
>
> —Shunryu Suzuki

Work

Brother Lawrence A Christian Zen Master

Recently, my monastery sent me to Burgundy to purchase wine for the community. I didn't want to go. I have no head for business, and I'm so lame the only way I can move around on the boat is by rolling myself over the wine casks. But I didn't fix my thoughts on my worries. Instead, I said to God, "This is Your business," and then I didn't give it another thought. And you know what? It all turned out fine.

> Imagine a man who comes home after a long, hard day's work in the fields, and sinks into his favorite chair in front of the fire. He has been working all day and he knows that he has achieved what he wanted to achieve; there is nothing more to worry about, nothing left unaccomplished, and he can let go completely of all his cares and concerns, content, simply, to be.
>
> —Dudjom Rinpoche

I hate kitchen work, but if I do everything for the love of God, with prayer, every moment of the day and night, then it all becomes easy. I've been working in the kitchen now for fifteen years, and by God's grace, I've done my work well. So I find satisfaction in my job—and yet I'd be willing to quit and do something else, because the details of whatever I'm doing, no matter what it is, can be offered up to God as love tokens. When I do that, I've discovered I please myself as well. I'm happy doing anything.

> If our heart is tormented
> because we are not able to accept
> things the way they are,
> then it is impossible to open our heart.
>
> —Anam Thubten

Brother Lawrence, A Christian Zen Master

When I have some task to do, something I would otherwise dread, I've learned not to worry about it ahead of time. When the time comes for the work to be done, I just look at God. It's like looking in the clearest mirror you could imagine, one that reveals the truth. When I look at God, I find in myself all I need for my work.

> When there is no "I," your
> mind is clear like space.
> Clear like space means clear like a mirror;
> clear like a mirror means a
> mind which just reflects:
> sky is blue, grass is green, water is flowing,
> sugar is sweet, salt is salty.
> The mirror-mind only reflects
> what's in front of it.
> In the mirror-mind what you
> see, what you hear,

Work

*what you smell, what you
taste, what you touch—
everything is just like this.
Just like this is truth.*

—Seung Sahn

When my external occupation makes me
less aware of my internal preoccupation
with God's presence, God gives me a
nudge. Then I'll find myself so on fire
with God, so lifted above my ordinary
life, that I can barely contain myself!
That's why I find myself more united
with God when I pray through my work
than when I pray alone in my cell.

There is no enlightenment outside of daily life.

—Thich Nhat Hanh

Brother Lawrence A Christian Zen Master

Becoming whole in mind and spirit, totally surrendered to God, does not mean that we have to stop doing the work we now do. Instead, what we once did for ourselves, to achieve our own ends, we now do for God. Our work is no longer our own; it belongs to God.

> They must not think that this world
> is meaningless and filled with confusion,
> while the world of Enlightenment
> is full of meaning and peace.
> Rather, they should taste the
> way of Enlightenment
> in all the affairs of this world.
>
> —the Buddha

People often confuse the end with the means. They think that certain kinds of work are more "holy" than others, and so they devote themselves to these actions, never realizing that they have attached their own selfish motivations to this "holy work."

> Enlightenment is not an achievement,
> it is an understanding that there
> is nothing to achieve.
>
> —Osho

Don't get tired of doing little things for the love of God. The size of our task matters not at all, only the love with which we do it.

> Before Enlightenment, chop
> wood, carry water.
> After Enlightenment, chop wood, carry water.
>
> —Zen proverb

Brother Lawrence *A Christian Zen Master*

Before I begin my work each day, I fill my mind with thoughts of the Infinite Being. Then I go through each step of the day, all that my work requires of me, and consider each task. When I think ahead like this, prayer fills up all the cracks in my day. Prayer begins my day, prayer ends my day. My personal experience of God never leaves me.

> When the task is done beforehand,
> then it is easy.
>
> —Yuan-tong

At the start of the workday, I come to God in loving surrender. I say to God, "Since You are with me now as I take up my work, turning my attention to the external affairs of my life, I ask You for the gift of Your Presence. Help me as I work, receive all that I do, take my love." As I continue with my work,

I continue my intimate conversation with God, asking for Divine grace, surrendering all that I do. Then, at the end of the day, I look back at the day and examine my work. Where I have done well, I thank God. Where I have failed, I ask forgiveness.

> If you are busy, then busyness
> is the meditation.
> Meditation is to know what you are doing.
> When you do calculations, know
> that you are doing calculations.
> If you are rushing to the office,
> then you should be mindful of "rushing."
> When you are eating, putting on your shoes,
> your socks, your clothes, you must be mindful.
> It is all meditation!
>
> —Dipa Ma

When we walk in the presence of God, the busiest moment of the day is no different from the quiet of a prayer altar. Even in the midst of noise and clutter, while people's voices are coming at you from all directions, asking for your help with many different things, you can possess God with the same serenity as if you were on your knees in church.

> Each place fills heaven and earth,
> every instant is eternal.
>
> —Sawaki Kôdô Rôshi

Direction

Brother Lawrence A Christian Zen Master

I know when I'm headed in the right direction because I can see the way ahead by the light of faith. This tells me that God is present, and so I keep going, my only goal always to simply please God, no matter what happens. This frees me from worrying so much about the consequences of my actions.

> The diminishing of your grasping is a sign that you are becoming freer of yourself. And the more you experience this freedom, the clearer the sign that the ego and the hopes and fears that keep it alive are dissolving and the closer you will come to the infinitely generous "wisdom of egolessness." When you live in that wisdom home, you'll no longer find a barrier between "I" and "you," "this" and "that," "inside" and "outside"; you'll have come, finally, to your true home.
>
> —Sogyal Rinpoche

I've tried seeking help from others—
but I always come away from our
conversations more confused than I
was to start with. All I do now is simply
commit myself to God. When we do
that, we have all the light we need to
show us how to live—and the journey
to heaven becomes simple and easy.

> On life's journey, faith is nourishment,
> . . . wisdom is the light by day and
> right mindfulness is the protection by night.
> If a person lives a pure life
> nothing can destroy her;
> If he has conquered greed
> nothing can limit his freedom.
>
> —the Buddha

Brother Lawrence A Christian Zen Master

My love for God is my only director.
I do my best to follow only that love,
so I have no need of outside guidance.

> *Our own mindfulness should be our teacher.*
>
> —Dudjom Rinpoche

Religion

Brother Lawrence A Christian Zen Master

The entire substance of religion consists of faith, hope, and love. As we practice these, we become one with God's will. Nothing else—all doctrine, all good works, all spiritual disciplines—matter very little. They are only means to the end. And that end is to be completely consumed by faith and love.

> Religion isn't an idea. It's practice.
>
> —Sawaki Kôdô Rôshi

The more you long for perfection—
to be whole and holy, utterly complete—
the more dependent you are on
Divine grace.

> When you eat, the meal becomes you.
>
> —Zen proverb

Religion

What is your goal in life? The only worthy goal is to become the most perfect worshippers of God we can possibly be, breathing in Divine worth as we breathe out praise.

> Ecstasy is our very nature;
> not to be ecstatic is simply unnecessary.
> To be ecstatic is natural, spontaneous.
> It needs no effort to be ecstatic,
> it needs great effort to be miserable.
> That's why you look so tired,
> because misery is really hard work.
>
> —Osho

Brother Lawrence A Christian Zen Master

A religious person told me recently that the spiritual life must begin with a servile fear that is increased by the hope of eternal life and is finally fulfilled by pure love. He said that each of these states has its owns stages, through which we must pass in order to arrive at holy perfection. But I have not followed these methods. I don't know why, but they made me feel discouraged. I decided to give up them all. I gave up even religion for God.

> Don't squeeze the way of
> Buddha into any frame.
>
> —Sawaki Kôdô Rôshi

Religion

When I first entered the religious life,
I thought I should spend my prayer
time thinking about my sins, about
death and judgment, about heaven and
hell, while the rest of the day, I simply
focused on God's presence. I thought
of God as always with me, often
within me. Gradually, almost without
noticing, I began to do the same thing
during my prayer times. I let go of
everything else. I stopped thinking
about theology and doctrine. I let go
of all of my ideas about God, so that
only faith was left. Only through faith
could I touch the infinite and incomprehensible God, a God that cannot be
contained by human ideas.

> "Empty theories" is what we call it
> when bystanders play around
> with terminology.
> Playing around like that is good for nothing.
> Dive in with body and soul!
>
> —Sawaki Kôdô Rôshi

For the first ten years, I worried that I was going about things in the wrong way. I didn't feel as though I deserved to be so happy or experience so much Divine grace, considering all my past sins. During this time, my spiritual life was filled with ups and downs. I felt as though circumstances, logic, even God were against me. Only faith was for me. I worried that I was being presumptuous, that I was simply pretending to have reached so easily a state of intimacy with God that others had worked so hard to achieve. Other times, I thought that I was deluding myself, that I had strayed far from the way of true religion. I thought I would spend the rest of my life like this—and yet at the same time, I remained completely surrendered, trusting God totally. Then my soul was suddenly at peace, as though she were at rest in the very center of her being. Ever since then, my religion is simply this: to do nothing and think nothing that is outside God. When I have done what I can, I pray God will be pleased to fill in the gaps.

Religion

Believe nothing on the faith of traditions,
even though they have been held in honor
for many generations and in diverse places.
Do not believe a thing because
many people speak of it.
Do not believe on the faith of
the sages of the past.
Do not believe what you
yourself have imagined,
persuading yourself that God inspires you.
Believe nothing on the sole authority
of your masters and priests.
But whatever, after due
examination and analysis,
you find to be kind, conducive to
. . . the welfare of all beings
that doctrine believe and cling to,
and take it as your guide.

—the Buddha

Brother Lawrence A Christian Zen Master

In holy inactivity,
abandoning all else,
we truly find God.
The soul in this state
desires nothing but God.
If I am deluded,
then I rely on God to remedy me.
I desire only God.

> Look within. Be still.
> Free from fear and attachment,
> know the sweet joy of living in the Way.
>
> —the Buddha

Love

Brother Lawrence A Christian Zen Master

Love is the rule by which I live.
And selfishness is the opposite of love.

> Being self-absorbed has an immediate effect of narrowing one's focus and blurring one's vision. It is like being pressed down by a heavy load. If, on the other hand, you think more about others' well-being, it immediately makes you feel more expansive, liberated and free.
>
> —the Dalai Lama

If we punish ourselves for our sins, and yet have no love, then what's the point? We don't need to worry about sin. Jesus Christ took care of sin, and now we shouldn't spend any time thinking about it. Instead, we should focus on learning to love God with all our being.

> Enlightenment, you see,
> is just another name for boundless love.
>
> —Anam Thubten

It's one thing to think about something and another to do it. Thinking about loving God is not the same as acting out our love. It doesn't really matter what we think, so long as we have made up our minds to act in a certain way.

> The foundation of all spiritual practice is love.
> That you practice this well is my only request.
>
> —the Dalai Lama

Ultimately, our only business in life is loving and delighting ourselves in God.

> With a boundless mind one could
> cherish all living beings,
> radiating friendliness over the entire world,
> above, below, and all around without limit.
>
> —Maitri Sutra

Brother Lawrence A Christian Zen Master

Consider this: You cannot love God if you do not know God. You cannot know God without coming into the Divine Presence. Once you come into the Presence, you will love God, for your heart will be with that which it values most.

> Understanding is the essence of love.
> If you cannot understand, you cannot love.
> That is the message of the Buddha.
>
> —Thich Nhat Hanh

Do not seek to love God for the way it makes you feel. Emotions, no matter how sweet or lofty, cannot bring us closer to God. Simply live in the Divine Presence. That is love. Cast everything else out of your mind.

> Love is a practice.
>
> —Thich Nhat Hanh

Love others without being attached to them. In other words, our love for others should never draw us from God. All else, including our love for our friends, should be surrendered to our love for God. When we do this, we need not fear the loss of those we love, for even in such loss, we are still in the Divine Presence.

> From what is loved, grief is born,
> from what is loved, fear is born.
> For someone freed from what is loved,
> there is no grief—
> so why fear?
>
> —the Buddha

Notes on the Buddhist Teachers

Ajahn Chah (1918–1992) helped establish the Thai Forest Tradition, a very ascetic form of Buddhism that has spread around the world.

The **Avatamsaka Sutra** is a collection of Buddhism's most sacred writings, compiled in the third or fourth century.

Buddhadhasa Bhikku (1906–1993) created an innovative reinterpretation of Buddhist doctrine and Thai folk beliefs that began a religious reformation in his home country of Thailand, as well as among Buddhists in other countries. Although Buddhadhasa was a formally ordained monk, he developed a personal view of the spiritual path that rejected specific religious identification. He considered all faiths as principally one.

The **Dalai Lama** is a Buddhist leader of a branch of Tibetan Buddhism. ("Lama" is a general term used to refer to Tibetan Buddhist teachers.) His followers believe him to be the rebirth of a long line of leaders who are considered to be manifestations of the enlightened being, Avalokite vara, who has chosen to be reborn in order to enlighten others with compassion.

Lama Surya Das (born as Jeffrey Miller in 1950) is an American-born spiritual teacher in the Tibetan Buddhist tradition. He is the author of many popular works on Buddhism and is a spokesperson for Buddhism in the West.

Dogen Zenji (1200–1253) was a Japanese Zen Buddhist teacher born in Kyoto, and the founder of the Sōtō school of Zen in Japan. He is known for his extensive writing, including the *Treasury of the Eye of the True Dharma*, concerning Buddhist practice and enlightenment.

Dudjom Rinpoche is the title of a line of spiritual teachers within Tibetan Buddhism. The most recent Dudjom Rinpoche was born in 1904 in Southern Tibet and died in 1987 in France. He was the head of a prominent Tibetan Buddhist school in exile.

Bhante Henepola Gunaratana is a Sri Lankan Buddhist monk (born in 1927) who came to the United States in 1968. He has taught graduate-level courses in Buddhism, as well as spiritual retreats, and he is the author of several books on Buddhism.

Ayya Khema (1923–1997) was born as Ilse Kussel in Berlin, Germany, to Jewish parents. She evaded the Nazis during World War II and eventually moved to the United States. After travelling in Asia, she decided to become a Buddhist nun in Sri Lanka in 1979. Throughout her lifetime, she helped create opportunities for women to practice Buddhism and wrote over two dozen books in English and German on Zen practice and the Buddha's teachings.

Jae Woong Kim is a Korean Buddhist monk who wrote *Polishing the Diamond, Enlightening the Mind*, a collection of his master's teachings on the quest for enlightenment.

Jack Kornfield (born 1945) is a popular American Buddhist teacher. He trained as a Buddhist monk in Thailand, Burma, and India, and was a student of the venerated Thai monk Ajahn Chah. He has taught Zen practice around the world since around 1974.

Dipa Ma (1911–1989) was a Buddhist master who chose home, work, and family over ascetic seclusion in a temple or monastery. She taught meditation and mindfulness amid everyday life from her apartment in Calcutta. Jack Kornfield and other American Buddhists were among her students.

The **Mahaparinirvana Sutra** is a sacred Buddhist text, written in the first and second centuries. It describes events from the life of the Buddha.

The **Maitri Sutra** is an ancient Buddhist sacred text that contains some of the words of the Buddha.

Thich Nhat Hanh (born in 1926 in Vietnam) is a Buddhist monk, teacher, author, poet and peace activist now based in France. He has been an important influence in the development of Western Buddhism.

Nyoshul Khenpo Rinpoche (1932–1999) was a Buddhist monk exiled from Tibet who was a master Zen teacher. He taught many of the prominent Buddhist leaders around the world.

Osho (1931–1990, also known as Bhagwan Shree Rajneesh) was a controversial Indian mystic and spiritual teacher who gained an international following. His teachings combined elements of many religious traditions, emphasizing the importance of meditation, awareness, love, celebration, creativity, and humor. In the last years of his life, his teaching focused on the practice of Zen.

Robert M. Pirsig (born in 1928) is an American writer and philosopher, and author of *Zen and the Art of Motorcycle Maintenance: An Inquiry into Values* (1974), a classic work that helped bring Zen to the attention of Americans.

Notes on the Buddhist Teachers

Seung Sahn (1927–2004) was a Korean Zen master who was one of the first Zen masters to settle in the United States. Known for his charismatic style and direct presentation of Zen, he opened many temples and practice groups around the world.

Sawaki Kôdô Rôshi (1880–1965) was an important Japanese Zen master.

Nyogen Senzaki (1876–1958) was a Zen monk who was one of the twentieth century's leading teachers of Zen Buddhism in the United States.

Shantideva was an eighth-century Buddhist scholar.

Shunryu Suzuki (1905–1971) was Japanese a Zen master who moved to the United States. The author of *Beginner's Mind*, he became one of the most influential Zen teachers in the Western world.

Sogyal Rinpoche (born 1947) is a Tibetan Buddhist who has been teaching Zen practice around the world for more than thirty years. He is also the founder and spiritual director of Rigpa, an international network of over a hundred Buddhist centers and groups in twenty-three countries around the world. He wrote the best-selling book *The Tibetan Book of Living and Dying*. He has been influential in interfaith dialogue, movements for peace and nonviolence, and hospice care for the dying.

Anam Thubten is a Buddhist monk from Tibet who has taught in the West. He is the author of *No Self, No Problem*.

Chogyam Trungpa (1937–1987) helped spread Tibetan Buddhism throughout the West.

Uchiyama Kosho Rôshi was Kodo Sawaki's closest disciple. He collected many of Sawaki's sayings, which have been published under the title *The Zen Teaching of "Homeless" Kodo*.

Thubten Lama Yeshe (1935–1984) was a Tibetan Buddhist teacher.

Yuan-tong was a Chinese Zen master.

The **Zenrinkusha** is an anthology of Chinese wisdom compiled in the seventeenth century.

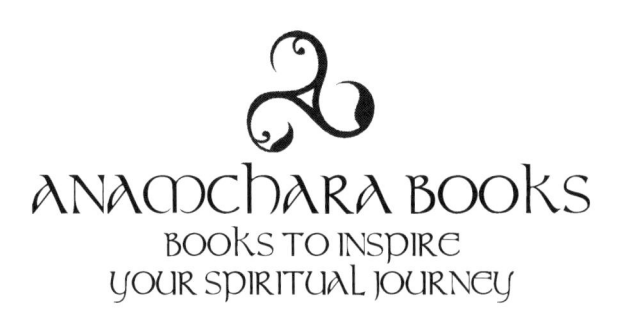

ANAMCHARA BOOKS
BOOKS TO INSPIRE
YOUR SPIRITUAL JOURNEY

In Celtic Christianity, an *anamchara* is a soul friend, a companion and mentor (often across the miles and the years) on the spiritual journey. Soul friendship entails a commitment to both accept and challenge, to reach across all divisions in a search for the wisdom and truth at the heart of our lives.

At Anamchara Books, we are committed to creating a community of soul friends by publishing books that lead us into deeper relationships with God, the Earth, and each other. These books connect us with the great mystics of the past, as well as with more modern spiritual thinkers. They are designed to build bridges, shaping an inclusive spirituality where we all can grow.

To find out more about Anamchara Books and order our books, visit **www.AnamcharaBooks.com** today.

ANAMCHARA BOOKS
Vestal, New York 13850
www.AnamcharaBooks.com

Printed in Great Britain
by Amazon